Passive Income:

40 Ideas to Successfully Launch Your Online Business

By: Adam Ovechkin

Table of Contents

information will be considered an illegal act irrespective of if it is done electronically or in print. This extends to creating a secondary or tertiary copy of the work or a recorded copy and is only allowed with an expressed written consent from the Publisher. All additional right reserved.

The information in the following pages is broadly considered to be a truthful and accurate account of facts and as such any inattention, use, or misuse of the information in question by the reader will render any resulting actions solely under their purview. There are no scenarios in which the publisher or the original author of this work can be in any fashion deemed liable for any hardship or damages that may befall them after undertaking information described herein.

Additionally, the information in the following pages is intended only for informational purposes and should thus be thought of as universal. As befitting

Introduction

Congratulations on downloading this book and thank you for doing so.

Who of us doesn't really enjoy getting rewarded for hard work? There is nothing more satisfying than being recognized for dedication and commitment to a task well done. There is a powerful sense of accomplishment and self-fulfillment that does more for building up the self-esteem of the person within than the financial rewards that many have offered.

At one time, it was the way of life for most people. When we were young, we were told that if we found a job dedicated 20 to 30 years of our lives to it, we would be rewarded with a pension that would carry us through the remainder of our days.

However, over the last few decades, we have witnessed that a concept makes a drastic change. Employers do not appreciate dedication like they used to. How often have we heard stories of someone being terminated only weeks before they were due to get their pensions? How many times have people committed to careers in companies only to find them forced to close their doors in the face of new technological innovations? How often has work in a traditional job been filled with unbelievable anxiety and stress, some to the point of causing major health problems for an employee?

This is not to say that the traditional way of work is nonexistent anymore. There are still plenty of people who have successfully made a go of it the old-fashioned way, but that number is quickly dwindling with each passing year.

With so many new types of technologies changing the way we do things, the idea of fighting rush hour traffic to sit in a cubicle or rushing to beat the clock every day is having less appeal, especially when you're not sure it will be there for the long haul.

The world we live in has changed and is poised to see a lot more changes in the very near future. If we hope to keep up with these constant changes, we need to embrace not just a new way to do things but a new way to think about them as well. In short, we need to learn the new rules of business. The good news is that in many cases, these new rules will offer more security, more enjoyment, and more satisfaction from the work we do now.

Whether you're looking for a little extra cash for spending money or you're looking to launch a whole new business to sustain you full time, there are many unique opportunities out there just for the taking. Many most people would not even think of because they are in niches that are far removed from the traditional way of earning money. The bottom line is there is money to be made, legitimate money that can enhance your current lifestyle or put you on a path to a whole new way of living.

In this book, we will discuss 40 different business ideas that can be done without ever leaving your home. New ways of working that will allow us to fill our lives much better than ever before.

Whether you want to work a 9-5 shift, or you just want to hit the keyboard whenever the mood strikes, there is a job out there that can help to seamlessly blend your personal life with your business life in a way that benefits everyone. In these pages, you'll learn the following:

- Jobs in sales and marketing
- Jobs in content marketing
- How to tap into your natural talents and make money off them
- How to earn a living as a freelancer
- How to use what you've got to get what you want
- And even how to get paid do what you always do

You'll be amazed at how different your view of work will be when you learn about the many work-at-home opportunities that are already available to you. We have entered a whole new world where age, gender, and educational status are no longer the primary deciding factor in how much money you can make. With the convenience of working from home, you can make as much or as little money as you want without someone else making these decisions for you. You can carve your own path, and you can create, build, and live your own dream without anyone judging you on your decisions.

If you're ready for this type of change and you're prepared to rethink the way you want to spend your days, it's time for us to get started. So, let's go.

There are plenty of books on this subject on the market, thanks again for choosing this one! Every effort was made to ensure it is full of as much useful information as possible, please enjoy!

Chapter 1: What Exactly is Passive Income?

From the time we are very small, we think of work as something that we must do to survive. We are told that if we work hard, perform well, and stick to it for the duration, we will be rewarded in our later years with a chance to relax and live life just as we've always wanted. It's a great dream, the American Dream, and we all believed it at some point in our life.

But the days we live in now are very different from the days of our parents and grandparents. Ironically though, it may be very similar to your third or fourth grandparents and their generation. During the years before the Industrial Revolution, most people worked for themselves. Whether you were a shoemaker or a baker, your sole source of income was from the work you did in your own home.

Today, however, after several hundred years of employer/employee relations, we've almost come full circle. We don't work for ourselves anymore, we work for money. Ask any number of people why they get up and head off to a job every day; inevitably, the clear majority of them will tell you that they work to make money; the more money they get, the better the job. At least that's what some people think.

However, when you work for yourself, there is a certain amount of satisfaction and self-fulfillment that cannot be measured in terms of dollars and cents. It reaches to the very heart of each of us.

Let me be clear at this point that when I use the words "passive income" in this book, I'm not referring to not working. I'm merely referring to another type of work, which is the kind where you can have the freedom to decide when and how much work you want to do.

Passive Income can be compared to nurturing an idea, a personal idea, or concept that encapsulates your dreams. You start small and let it build up over time until it has become viable enough to support you in the life you want to lead. It is income that is generated once and continues to produce money long after the work is finished.

Unlike active income, which requires you to work continuously to get paid, passive income results from an initial investment of effort but, once started, will require minimal effort to generate income. If you work the usual 9-5 shift and are paid by the hour, your income stops growing when you quit work for the day, but with passive income, it will continue to grow even while you're sleeping.

What passive income is not, however, is a get rich quick scheme where you are promised that if you spend a little money, you'll get tons more. Those types of high-risk schemes rarely pay off and, in most cases, never will.

Some may argue that these kinds of incomes are not guaranteed, and you could lose a lot more than you earn in the process. This is true; there are risks involved with anyone who is trying to step out on his own. However, is anyone guaranteed a continuous paycheck when they sign on for a regular employer/employee relationship? Not likely. In fact, with so many businesses struggling to keep up with the constant changes in the different industries, there are no guarantees anyway. Every day we hear of companies closing, declaring bankruptcy, and people losing jobs they have been on for years. And those that do manage to survive are not offering salaries that are keeping up with the rate of inflation, so even if there is no change, you are still losing money.

This is not to say that there is no risk involved with passive income opportunities, but it is something that, with the proper managing, effective planning, and taking the necessary precautions, can be minimized. The upside is that if done right, there is a payout in your future, not to mention a chance for you to call your own shots and control your source of income in the process.

So, now is the time to stop making someone else richer and turn that same energy you give to your employer to yourself so that you can reap the true benefits of all your hard work.

There are several ways to do this, some of them obvious, and others may not be so easily identified. And now, with the advent of the World Wide Web, it is possible to accomplish all your goals without ever having to leave your home. So, let's get started.

Chapter 2: Getting in the Right Mindset for Passive Income

Before you can implement any plan to generate passive income, you need to prepare yourself mentally. The good news is that most of these opportunities will cost you nothing or very little money, so you won't be put on hold while you work to make the money to get started. That will come later, but you won't need it to get started. What you do need though is the right mindset to keep you on track.

Your Dream

The primary core of any type of venture must come from within. We've all had a dream of being an independent person at some point in our lives. Whether we're a child setting up a lemonade stand in front of our house or we're working on a job that is full of drudgery, our thoughts will inevitably drift off to better times.

Think back on your life and try to pull up some of those dreams you've had in the past. The heart of those dreams should serve as the impetus to determining what type of passive income will interest you the most. There are thousands of ways to generate this type of income, but chances are, the methods that will have a better chance of being successful will start with the dreams you have had throughout your life.

For example, if you have always had a dream of writing your own book and making a living as a writer, you should follow that spirit. To open an online store for selling merchandise will likely generate income for you but not likely fuel your inner spirit like writing a book would.

With so many options for creating a passive income for yourself, it is more important than ever that you focus on those dreams that motivate you. Later, as we discuss the different ideas, some will ring true and strike that inner chord to motivate you. Those are the ones you should focus your attention on and will have the best chance of success for you.

Your Plan

Next, you must start setting some goals for yourself. Start by creating short, medium, and long-term goals. It is okay to say you want to be independent in one year, but you must set your sites on something a bit more practical. Being financially independent is an ideal goal, but it won't provide you with enough incentive to move forward in your strategy. You need to take your goal-making strategies and take them a step further.

To do that, you need to make smaller and smaller goals. For example, if you want to be financially independent in one year, decide what steps you need to take to accomplish that. You could set up regular milestones perhaps set at 3, 6, and 9 months. When that is finished, take your first milestone at 3 months and break that up into smaller milestones, perhaps three separate goals, one for each month.

Then you could go even further by taking your monthly goal and breaking it up into weekly milestones, then do the same on the weekly basis, and again at the daily basis. Finally, break it down to the 1-day plan, which could be divided up into smaller 1-hour targets.

Now, your plan is broken down into small, bite-sized pieces that are very realistic to follow. This way, your big goal of being financially independent won't seem so far out of reach and will feel like it is very much within your realm of possibilities.

There are a few things you need to keep in mind when you create your goals.

- Each goal must be specific so that you know exactly what you're working for.

- Each goal must be measurable so that you know if you have achieved it.
- Each goal must be achievable so that you know it is possible.
- Each goal must be realistic so that you believe it is within your reach.
- Each goal must have a time frame so that you have boundaries.

To help you recall these guidelines, use the acronym S.M.A.R.T.

Specific
Measurable
Achievable
Realistic
Timed

If each of your goals meets all these requirements, then you have a plan that is ready to implement.

Your Fortitude

Next, you want to prepare for what others may say or do that could affect your reaching your goals. The idea of generating a passive income is not always appreciated by well-intentioned family members and friends. They may believe that the steps you are about to take are just too risky and try to talk you out of your well-thought-out plan. However, while their words may be tempting, you need to make a commitment to it to succeed.

Some people decide to overcome these types of obstacles simply by keeping it a secret and not telling anyone of your plans until they have already achieved some level of success. Others choose to only tell those who are most likely to give them the support they need to help them to accomplish their goals. And some just choose to tell everyone and brace themselves for the fallout. Whatever you choose to do, don't be surprised to find that most people are not willing to join the fun until they see the results for themselves, so you may have to go it alone in the beginning. But remember, this will be a fulfillment of your personal dreams and not theirs so make sure that you only take the advice of someone you want to trade places with.

So, if your dream is to set up your own online dress store, the advice you should listen to should come from someone with a similar dream and drive. Listening to a happy housewife with five kids underfoot will only discourage you. Her dreams and yours are not in alignment; therefore, she will neither understand what you're trying to do and most likely not understand your personal drive to change.

If you're in doubt about any step in your plan, make sure that you ask someone who is capable of not only understanding your business but also your goals. And don't expect everyone in your life to be on board. If you have a question about some avenue of your new venture, always, always, always make sure you ask the right people.

You will make mistakes and you will have setbacks. But rather than have these situations to derail your plans, decide beforehand that you will use each of them as stepping stones to a more successful venture the next time. Rather than let those mistakes defeat you, use them to move you forward, get up, and try again.

As I've said before, this is not a get rich quick scheme nor is it a plan that does not require any work. Passive income requires an investment of time. That is why your detailed plan that we've discussed earlier is so perfect. Because you've divided the job up into smaller, bite-sized pieces, the mistakes that you make in the very beginning will be small and won't cost you as much. But as you master your initial skills, your ability to navigate your plan will improve and you'll be surprised at the strides you'll make.

Advantages of Passive Income

A word of caution is warranted here. The idea of being your own person, free from the encumbrances of a boss dictating your every move can be quite appealing. It is one of the biggest draws for most people seeking a passive income. We've watched them in movies where the whole concept of building your own empire and surpassing that of your boss is beyond desirable. The ability to tell him or her where to "stick it" has crossed the minds of all of us.

Who wouldn't want to get up every morning and walk barefoot from their bedroom to their workspace in their pajamas and flip on the computer to make a few bucks? This is a major advantage of a passive income. You can live and be pretty much anywhere in the world and make your money. So, whether you want to lounge at the beach or climb to the highest mountain peaks, your income will continue to flow in wherever you are.

Another huge advantage that comes from generating a passive income is the free time you will have. In the beginning, you can fully expect that you will do a lot of work, but over time, as your reputation is spread among your potential customer base, you will see that you need to work less and less to achieve your goals. Rather than committing all your time to an employer who wants to pay you only a small payment for the hour, you can dictate when you want to work, how much time you dedicate to any project, and exactly when you're ready to walk away.

Once it is all set up, most passive income jobs can run themselves. You won't need to monitor it every minute, and once all the bugs are out of your system, you can simply check in periodically to update it or monitor your strategies as the money rolls in. What you do with all that extra time you have is entirely up to you.

There will never be a need for you to get permission to take off for a vacation ever again.

Disadvantages

There are also some disadvantages to a passive income that you need to prepare for. It is not without its own share of work. You will be starting your own business, which means that you are going to be the sole party responsible for what happens in your business. If you're not accustomed to wearing many hats, this may not be the best choice for you.

Even if you choose to do a job that requires a one-time investment of time, there will always be monitoring and maintenance issues that will have to be dealt with. While we do use the term "passive," do not expect that you won't ever have to dedicate time to keeping your income going. There will always be things you'll have to do to keep things running smoothly.

For example, if you do get the income streams you're hoping for, you may have to enlist the aid of an accountant to keep the records straight. No one gets away without having to pay Uncle Sam his due. You'll have to stay in communication with your customers, and you'll need to keep updating the work you've already done; otherwise, your clients may become bored and lose interest. When that happens, you lose money too.

Also, whatever industry you choose to work with, you will need to keep abreast of how it's evolving so that your business will stay in-tune. This means doing additional research and maybe even taking a few classes to keep you competitive.

It won't be passive in the beginning. In fact, it'll be very busy when you first get started. If you're not willing to put in the time up front, there is little chance that you'll produce a steady stream of income later.

Expect things to happen that are completely out of your realm of control. These could be factors like the economy, the introduction of new technology, lack of buyer interest, or even a new Google algorithm that moves your position around the search engines. To put it simply, a passive income is never guaranteed, and anything can happen to change it, stop it, or just slow it down, and you'll need to change your tactics to keep your income going. You may not be able to foresee and prepare for everything, but what you can prepare for is the fact that inevitably things will change, and you'll have to have the spirit needed to adapt as time goes on.

Finally, you need some guts; some deep down, intestines of steel guts that will help you to stay the course against all odds. You also need self-discipline to keep you on the right track. This is a lesson on passive income, not an I'll get to it when I feel like it income. You may find that you must do 50- or 60-hour weeks before you can get to the 5-hour week and find time to relax on the beach.

And you can fully expect that if you are successful, you will have to work even harder. There may be many skeptics when you first strike out on your own, but in time, when those same skeptics see your success, you can fully expect them to reemerge as your competitors. Everyone wants a piece of the money pie, but few of them are willing to openly admit it.

Now that you have a pretty good picture of what is expected of you, it is time for you to decide just where you stand on the passive income picture. Many are likely going to step aside, deciding once and for all that this type of work is not for them and that would be fine. It is much better for you to learn and understand this fact before you start and end up sinking a lot of time and money into the venture. However, there will be just as many, if not more, who are even more excited about the possibilities and is ready to jump in with both feet.

Chapter 3: How to Get Started

When it comes to passive income, it can start any number of ways. One mistake newbies often make is to choose work that promises to generate a lot of money in a short amount of time. While there is nothing wrong with that, it is important for you to understand that you likely will not have anyone behind you, pushing you and driving you forward with your plans. If you have no passion for your job, then you'll likely lose your enthusiasm over time and your zeal for the money will soon fade out. At that time, the drudgery of the job will lose its interest, and your goals will probably begin to fail.

The best advice I can give you when it comes to choosing which path you will take to passive income is to follow your dreams. This is a crucial factor that will contribute greatly to your success. To get started, you will need to spend many hours planning, developing, and building up your new venture, and if you don't absolutely love what you're doing, you could easily lose interest and eventually quit. You must have a passion so that you can enjoy what you're doing.

The key to your success does not lie in how much money you must invest, nor does it matter how many connections you must help you get ahead. It lies in how much you know about your chosen field. Statistics show that those who have more knowledge and have developed more skills are more likely to succeed in their ventures than someone who just picks up something because of the potential money. Choose a venture that you can see yourself dedicating every fiber of your being into it, and your odds of generating long-term income can be quite high. It won't be an immediate success, but once everything falls into place, it will be something you will appreciate for many years.

How to Choose a Passive Income Opportunity

One of the first things you need to do is to take to the Internet to find the right opportunity for you. The Internet is chocked full of great ideas, but you must be careful. Not everything promised is for real, and many of them can be scams. Remember, if it sounds too good to be true, chances are it really is too good to be true. While scrutinizing opportunities that may not be all they are cracked up to be, look for an idea that offers something that will appeal to a clear majority of people. While it may be a good idea to look for something that appeals to you, it must also can draw in a lot of people.

For example, perhaps your hobby is making silk flowers. You love this work more than anything in the world, but if you don't have a significant group of people to serve as your customer base, no matter how passionate you may feel about it, you'll have a hard time getting sales. Look for something that offers enough value to your potential customer base, and you'll be halfway to your goal.

With that thought in mind, it is now time to tickle your brain to come up with some ideas of your own. Here are some suggestions that will help you to make the best decision for your personal ideals, circumstances, and goals.

Chapter 4: 40 Awesome Ideas for Passive Income

Idea #1—Write a Book

There is a saying that inside everyone, there is a story to be told. No matter who you are, where you come from, or your personal background, there is something about your life that will appeal to someone else. We live in a world where we are all connected in ways our ancestors would have never been able to imagine. Where at one time in the past, it was only possible to share your experiences with a small inner circle, with today's modern technology, you can share your story with millions in a matter of seconds.

No matter what your story is, you can rest assured that someone out there wants to know it. But in writing your story, there are two challenges you must face. The first you have total control over, how to write it. If you don't have unique writing skills, then the next best thing for you to do is to hire a ghostwriter to help you tell your story. Your second challenge is to find your audience, which may require you to learn a few marketing strategies or hire someone to make sure to get the word out.

If you don't want to tell your personal story, that's okay, you could also sell your personal expertise in a specific area. The number of self-help books out there will amaze you, and the potential for you to help millions of people is just a few steps away. If you're skilled in any specialty, writing about it and giving people step-by-step guides can earn you lots of money. Here's how you do it.

1. Choose your niche—when deciding on what to write about, think of a problem common to people in your field. When you write your book, make sure that you tell them the answer to that problem and you will likely have a customer for

life. You can also think about any subcategories where there is not much information available to help people. For example, you might want to address the subject of how to find a good idea for a money-making business, or it could be something as simple as what is the secret to a fluffy and light low-calorie cake. Make sure that the title is intriguing enough to get people to take a second look and you're on your way. If you're not sure of a profitable idea to write about, check out Amazon's top 100 books and that should get your mental juices flowing.

2. Do research—Yes, you may know your subject, but there are always new ideas coming up every day. Do your research to find out what new industry trends are in the making so that you can incorporate these new ideas into your business. You will quickly notice that the most popular topics will have several

books already addressing it. Look over those books and try to tailor your book so that it approaches the same subject but from a different angle. Don't forget to read the reviews and comments people have made and make sure that you glean the best dos and don'ts when you write your book.

3. Create a professional image—Every book needs a good cover and a marketing strategy. You might think you can do it yourself but having a professionally designed cover can do wonders for your book sales. And don't assume that because you have a good grammar that your book is picture perfect. Invest in a professional editor to make sure that it will appeal to the write audience and to catch those mistakes every writer inevitably misses.

4. Publish the book—The good news is that publishing your book is easier than ever now. You can simply upload the book on Amazon and have it available in 12 countries in less than 24 hours. This means you will be open for business in a very short period and bringing in the money.

5. Market the book—Your final step is to market the book. Now, if you have good marketing skills, you can take care of this step yourself, but for the most part, if you're a good writer, then chances are you are weak in marketing. By hiring a professional to do that kind of work for you, there are plenty of people that will be more than happy to help you. Finding your target audience can be done through a wide range of sources including social media, blogging, and other promotions. It may take a while for your name to get out

there, but once it does, your money will start flowing in.

Idea #2—Selling Data

Every year, more and more businesses are keenly interested in collecting data to help them to target their potential clientele. By agreeing to collect the data they need, you can easily earn a hundred or more dollars per month of passive income.

To that end, most companies are willing to buy information to help them to achieve their goals. The trick is to find which companies are willing to pay for the information you can collect or already have in your possession. While you may not have access to other people's personal data, you can easily sell details about your personal experiences as a means of making money.

Every day, other companies sell personal information about you to these same businesses, and when they do, you have no control over what information gets out and who has it. But with this method, you have complete control over which companies you want to sell your information to and what information you want them to have.

There are several websites you can use to connect to companies willing to pay for your information. These include the following:

Nielson—
https://mobilepanel.nielsen.com

They pay around $50/year in gift cards, and you can get yourself set up in less than an hour. You simply download their application into your mobile device, and it will collect all your data as you use it. The application is designed to collect information on how you use your device, when you use it, and how often you play games and which apps you use.

It does not collect personal information or anything that might be considered remotely sensitive. It will, however, collect your name, address, email, gender, age, and your current location, but this information is purely for purposes of determining market trends and who is interested in what products. All the data will be uploaded to the Nielson site automatically, so once your device is set up, there is nothing left for you to do. Nielson's goal is only to track information on how you best use your device and nothing else.

You earn points that can be accumulated and converted into gift cards, which can be exchanged for all sorts of electronic items.

AppOptix—
http://panel.strategyanalytics.com/

If you have an Android, you could also sign up with AppOptix. Their app runs in the background of your device, so once you're set up, there is nothing else for you to do. If they can collect enough information from your device at the end of the year, you will receive a $50 Amazon gift card. They do have rather strict criteria, but if you match their needs, it is easy money. Simply, download the application, respond to their email confirmation, and complete their profile form.

It works on the point system. For every week, you run the application you receive a hundred points, and for every 300 points, you receive a $10 Amazon gift card. These can be accumulated until you reach a maximum of $50 for the year.

Datacoup—https://datacoup.com

Datacoup targets your social media activity and transaction fees that you accumulate with your debit and credit cards. Through them, you can provide your banking information, debit and credit card usage, and any other online accounts you may use to purchase anything.

It is important to understand that the company does not collect or sell any information that may personally identify you. They are only interested in charting the trends and activities you may use to purchase goods. Once all your information is connected and your profile is created, they will have a good overview of your data, which they can then resell to those businesses that are looking specifically for different buyer groups. Once your data is bought, you will receive payment, which is sent directly to your bank account or your debit card.

There are several other companies that will do the same. The payout is minimal, but if you're connected to enough of them, you can earn a decent annual income. Once you're set up, there is nothing else for you to do. You simply continue just as you would normally and get paid for it.

Idea #3—Amazon FBA

Almost everyone has heard of Amazon, but few people know what Amazon FBA is, but if you have any plans of selling specific merchandise, this might be the absolute easiest way to get your products into the hands of the consumer without having to worry about shipping, handling, or marketing. It works best for those businesses that have difficulty warehousing a large quantity of any product.

FBA simply means fulfilled by Amazon, and since they house your products on site, once you have delivered it to Amazon, there is nothing left for you to do but collect the money. It is important, however, to make sure that it is the right arrangement for you and for your customer base. But using Amazon to connect you to your customer is one of the easiest marketing strategies you can have. With their already large customer base, you will likely reach far more potential customers than you might ever do on your own.

You simply set up your own Amazon account, scan your list of products into the system, print out the barcodes, a packing slip, and then choose a pick-up location based on where you live, and in just a few days, your products are safely stored in the Amazon warehouse. All you must do at that point is wait for the orders to be placed and the money to roll in.

The benefits of this arrangement are obvious. You not only get easy access to the millions of consumers that log into Amazon every day, but you also save time and money in shipping items to different places around the world. Amazon covers the storage of your merchandise and the shipping costs related to it. If you choose a relatively popular item, you stand to earn quite a bit of money on simply reselling the merchandise you were already planning on selling anyway.

Idea #4—Online Shopping Portals

These are relatively easy to set up and get started. You may not earn a great deal, but you can easily see your way to clear to about $15/month or more from each site you choose to connect with.

By linking to online shopping portals like Ebates or TopCashBack, you can earn commissions from purchasing products from their listed websites. Since the average household spends around $7000 a year on household goods, there is a lot of potential for some major profits. By using an online shopping portal, you can generate a tidy little passive income doing exactly what you would normally do.

With Ebates, you can shop at more than 2000 different stores collecting rebates as you go. The amount of money you receive could vary depending on which promotional codes you use and the items you purchase.

Simply by joining Ebates, you can accumulate hundreds of coupons offering you cash back on your purchases. You might be wondering how you can make money on rebates for things you purchase. This only works if you're purchasing things you were already planning on purchasing, to begin with. You can collect rebates over time and use them to your advantage.

You can also use these items for resale if you have no intention of using them for your own personal benefits. In many cases, they will issue you a check every few months, and in other cases, you might receive payment within a few weeks. If you purchase items for resale, you have two different ways to generate a passive income.

Idea #5—Make Money with Videos

You've probably already heard about how many people are making home videos, uploading them to YouTube and collecting lots of money in the process. With the right know-how, you can generate income for yourself as well. However, there are some things you must already have in place to make this type of plan work.

For this to work, you cannot rely solely on your smartphone camera. You need to have quality equipment to get the best results. This means you'll need a camera dedicated to recording, a good microphone, and the right lighting situation. This might require an initial outlay of cash to get started, but once you do, you can generate quite a bit of income.

It is also a good idea for you to have a website that people can connect to. Your own website can generate a great deal of money for YouTubers. Those who enjoy your videos can connect directly to your site for more information. This site, in turn, can link to your Facebook or Twitter page.

You can create a video on just about anything you might think of. If you feel you are good at any topic that might appeal to others, you'll find that creating a video can be a great tool. Many people would prefer to see a 10-minute video on something they want to know rather than reading an article or book on the same subject.

Your goal in creating a video should be on giving your audience something they wouldn't otherwise learn or understand from other sites. To make this avenue a success, there are several things you must keep in mind when making your videos.

1. Target a specific audience.
2. Don't make it too long, get to the point quickly.

3. Be enthusiastic—avoid the tendency to talk slow and give your audience some energy.
4. Be unique—the more successful videos offer something that no one else has.

If you plan your video content carefully and think about your audience, you have a good chance of a successful venture. It is astonishing to know how much money can be made from a successful YouTube video. While YouTube does not pay you directly for any video content you upload to their site, when your video gains traction, you will create a following, which can generate income in and of itself. In addition, you will attract the attention of advertisers who will be more than happy to piggyback on your success and pay you for the privilege.

The important thing to remember is that you must be unique. No one will pay you for something that everyone else is doing. The more you can stand out from the crowd, the more money there is in your future. If you make your views informative and entertaining, you will eventually attract a following that can generate lots of money for your future.

Also, look for something with viral appeal. In other words, you want something that will compel people to share the information with others. This will help to spread your name around the YouTube community generating additional income for you as it goes.

It is important to understand that to generate a steady stream of income, you will need to put up videos on a regular basis. Whether this is weekly or monthly, the more consistent you are with delivery, the more reliable you'll be, attracting more and more people to your site on a regular basis. Whether you choose to release a video once a week or once a month, make sure that you stick to your schedule and do not waver. The more loyal you are to your viewers, the more money you will make.

Idea #6—Viewing Ads and Collecting Rewards

This is a very simple and easy way to generate additional income. There are many companies that are more than happy to pay for referrals and your ability to share their content with other users. Each time you post about a product or service you can be paid in the form of rewards.

You might be wondering why anyone would pay for you to do this. The answer is simple. Anytime you tell someone about their product or service, it generates income for them. In most cases, if the customer is satisfied, they will return again and again to the same business. So, while they may have to pay you some sum of money to bring new business to their doors, the next time that same customer buys from them, it is pure profit.

To put it simply, you are helping them to reach their target audience and spread their message to those who they want to draw into their inner circle. It's a win-win situation for everyone; businesses get to grow their customer base, users can find quality products more easily, and you get a few extra bucks in your pocket.

If this sounds like something that you can get excited about, then your chances of making money are good. On average, you can generate around $150/month with this strategy, and it is usually easy to get started. Here are just two companies that you can start with.

> Perk TV: http://www.getperk.com/
> Swagbucks:
> https://www.swagbucks.com/refer/n
> oone2das

Idea #7—Airbnb Search Engine Optimization

If you have the property that you can rent out on a temporary basis, this is an easy way to get a little extra cash in your pocket. Most people think of Airbnb as a travel site where they can find affordable places to rent that are homier. Few realize that it is a search engine designed to look for rooms and apartments for rent rather than websites.

For this reason, having a little knowledge in search engine optimization can help immensely in getting your property ranked higher on the list. Once your property is listed, if you make sure you're always available to respond to requests, answer questions, and offer a quality set-up, you'll start moving up your ranking and can potentially generate a nice sum of passive income in the process.

Idea #8—Create a Niche Website

With so many copycat ideas for businesses, creating something that's just a little off from the norm can cause quite a buzz and attract a lot more interest. By offering a product or service that is not another copy of the same old thing can generate a lot of income.

In coming up with a unique idea, try to think of offering something that will have a wide appeal for your target customer. Your concept must go beyond the obvious. An online store for women's clothes is not necessarily a good idea, but an online store for hard to fit women would be a nice niche. Online shoe stores are everywhere but what about an online shoe store that only offers large sizes.

To have a niche website, its content has to offer something that your potential customers may not be able to get easily in other places. You won't be marketing to the masses, but you can corner a nice niche market for those who may not be able to easily shop at the other sites thus locking in a loyal customer base that won't be able to go somewhere else as easily.

The trick here is to find a problem or a need in the community and use your website to fill that need. Once your product is chosen and the site is set up, with the right marketing techniques, you can easily generate a steady stream of income with little to no effort.

Idea #9—Drop Shipping

The beauty of drop shipping is that it is a fast and easy way to turn a buck. With products being developed and shipped all over the world, the drop shipper can connect the supplier with the consumer without ever leaving their home. You simply advertise the product to the potential customer, when the order comes in collect the payment and notify the supplier where to ship the product.

With this type of business, you simply serve as the middleman. You do not have to warehouse a lot of goods nor do you ever need to handle the product at all. Your primary focus is on advertising and promoting the different products you sell.

With the right website, you can drop ship hundreds of different products this way and never have to worry about packaging, storage, or shipping hassles. The supplier never has to worry about marketing his products or finding his customer base. There is no limit to how much you could make with this type of business venture.

One of the great things about drop shipping is that you will never have to invest a great deal of money into inventory to get started. However, there are some drawbacks and challenges to drop shipping you need to prepare for. Make sure that you connect with legitimate suppliers so that you're not caught in the middle of a scam. And make sure that they are reliable and trustworthy. Even legitimate companies do not always have the best of reputations.

Idea #10—Blogging

Blogging is an excellent way to make some easy money. If you have decent writing skills and you have something to say that would appeal to a lot of people, there is a great way to earn a little cash in your free time.

Look online and you'll find all sorts of people are blogging now. Advice columns are now the order of the day, so you'll find opinions posted from students in school to CEOs of major corporations. You can think of blogging as the backyard fence that people talked over many years ago.

Not only is this a profitable venture, it is also very fun and exciting as you develop your own following. If you're thinking about creating your own blog, however, there are a few things you need to consider carefully before you start.

First, determine who will be your target audience and learn everything you can about them. These are the people you will be speaking to when you write your blog. The more you know about them, the easier it will be for you to tailor your conversation to something that will appeal to them.

Once you've decided on your topic and have researched your target audience, all you must do is set up a pleasing and professional website so that your blog will be presented in a nice package. If you don't have skills in website design, it might be a good idea to hire someone to do it for you. It may cost you more up front, but you'll eventually get that back in time.

Then all you must do is to promote your blog to your audience. You can do this by linking your blog to a variety of social media platforms and encourage your followers to share it with their friends.

You won't make money with a blog in the beginning, but after you have developed a sizable following, it will attract advertisers who will want to be a part of your blogging system and you'll be slowly bringing in the cash. After that, you'll just have to write new blog posts on a regular basis, and the site will run itself, generating passive income for you as you go.

Idea #11—Affiliate Marketing

For those who may already have a sizable following in social media, affiliate marketing may be a great way to generate passive income. While you can still do it with a smaller following, it may take you longer to generate the kind of income you're looking for if you must build up an audience at the same time.

Affiliate marketing is simply connecting buyers to online products. By recommending these products to people, you automatically earn a commission on every sale that is made. The process is very simple.

- The buyer seeks to buy an item.
- He visits an online affiliate site.
- The affiliate marketer recommends a product and links the buyer to the merchant's site.
- The buyer purchases the product, and the affiliate receives his commission.

By setting up an affiliate site with a merchant, your website can virtually run itself. Most online companies offer some form of affiliate program so that you can easily sign up and get started. Whether you have a blog where you make your recommendations, or you have a website designed to showcase affiliate products, you can easily generate income with only a little effort.

To get set up, you simply sign up on their website, and they will give you a unique link you will use when you recommend their products. When visitors come to your site, they will click on that link, and if they decide to buy, you will receive a commission. It may take some time before your reputation and credibility are accepted by the masses, and until then, your commissions could be very low at best, but if you persist and keep at it, eventually your income could grow to the point of allowing you to be self-sufficient.

The most successful affiliate marketers are those who choose a specific niche and stick to it, they are diligent at marketing their own website and are willing to work with several vendors to compound their chances at profit.

Idea #12—Selling Photos

If you are a pretty good photographer, there may be money to be found in selling your photos. If you're already posting a lot of photos on sites like Instagram, you could be well on your way to a tidy little profit. Most people have some great photos already saved on their computers and smartphones, so getting started should be very easy.

There are quite a few websites like Shutterstock.com and iStockphoto.com that offer a platform for you to sell your photos. With these sites, the more photos you have in your portfolio, the larger potential for returns there are.

You do not need to be a professional photographer; even amateurs who are just learning their way around a camera can contribute. Simply, visit each site and apply as a contributor. Once accepted, you can immediately begin to upload your photos and start generating income.

Not all photos are accepted though, so to make sure that your photos are not rejected, here are a few things to keep in mind.

- Avoid taking pictures of people you don't know

- Make sure that your images do not have name brand products featured
- Offer a variety of sizes
- Clean up any pixilated or grainy areas in the photo
- Offer a variety of different themes

Here is a list of several sites that will accept photos for sale:

Fotolia.com
Makeuseof.com
SmugMug.com
iStockPhoto.com
Photocrati.com
Shutterstock.com
TourPhotos.com
BlueMelon.com
Alamy.com
DreamsTime.com
Zenfolio.com
Flickr.com
Fotomoto.com
PhotoDune.net
Canstockphoto.com
123rf.com

FineArtAmerica.com
Crestock.com
500px.com
ArtStorefronts.com

Of course, there are a lot more sites you can choose from, but these will be perfect to get you started.

Idea #13—Become an Amazon Mechanical Turk

These are sometimes referred to as micro jobs. They are small insignificant tasks that anyone can do. These are usually tasks that computers have not yet mastered, so they still must be performed by humans. For example, computers have still not developed to the point of analyzing images. You may be assigned to tag objects found in an image, help a company select the best picture for a product marketing campaign, audit images, and videos for quality content or classify or identify objects in satellite imagery.

But images are not the only things Mechanical Turks can do. You may be hired to gather information, fill out market research data, or transcribe audio content. The fact is that there are lots of ways a Mechanical Turk can be used, and it should be very easy to find a job that matches with your skills.

To apply, simply visit https://www.mturk.com/worker and fill out the form.

Idea #14—Teaching Online Classes

Another excellent way to generate passive income is by teaching online courses. There are several sites that will allow you to create a video class featuring your unique set of skills or talent in any area of your personal expertise.

If you enjoy creating content and teaching people what you know, then this could turn out to be very profitable for you. Whether you are an expert guitarist, or you have the secret to baking the perfect cake, you can generate your own following and teach people what you know.

Udemy is one of the best places to get started with teaching your courses, but there are other sites as well. Whether you want to teach technical courses that focus on something complicated or you want to explain some skill that is hard for people to acquire, you can end up with a global classroom with thousands of people willing to learn what you have to offer. To get started with Udemy, visit https://www.udemy.com/teaching/?ref =teach_header and sign up.

Through them, you can share all your knowledge and talents to a whole world of students and generate a nice little income at the same time. The beauty of it is that once the video is made, it will continue to generate income for as long as you keep it up there.

Idea #15—Become a Virtual Assistant

It is important to understand that becoming a virtual assistant won't generate a lot of money, but if you live in an area that doesn't have a high cost of living, it is a great way to generate some easy income. Many people who like to travel will take advantage of this type of job because they can easily tap into the Internet and work from anywhere in the world.

If you have access to the reliable Internet and a good computer system, working as a virtual assistant can be ideal. You will, however, need to be reliable, good at communicating, and able to work independently. Your ability to stick to a schedule and meet deadlines will take you a long way in this type of work.

To find jobs as a virtual assistant, you can upload a profile on sites like

Upwork.com, Freelancer.com, and Indeed.com.

Idea #16—Outsourcing Your Skills

If you have a special skill or talent that you can do online, you don't need to have an employer to hire you. You can freelance your way to a pretty good income instead. In fact, offering your skills for special jobs like writing, editing, graphic designing, computer programming, and a host of other skills is in high demand right now.

When you're searching for a job, you are marketing your skills to an employer, but if you consider yourself your own employer, you can make yourself available to a host of interesting projects. Once started, rather than waiting for an employer to give you a raise, you can give it to yourself. The more successful freelancers eventually do well enough to hire their own staff so that the business can run itself and they can take a back seat and still make money.

There are quite a few freelancing sites available that for a percentage of your earnings will happily connect you with a host of potential clients. Visit sites like Upwork.com and Freelancer.com to get started. Over time, you will eventually find that if you do good work, you could easily have a steady stream of income coming in.

This idea can even work even if you don't have a special skill. Simply by hiring those that do you can start your own business and farm out the work to those who do. This works best if you at least have good managerial skills to keep it all together.

The ability to tap into the talents of others is the ideal way to generate a good and steady passive income.

Idea #17—Become a Captcha Solver

It is easy to increase your online income by working as a captcha solver. The task is easy. All you must do is read the captcha images and type in the exact characters that you read. It doesn't pay a lot of money, but if you are fast, you can still bring in a little spending cash when you need it. The pay averages about $2 for every 1000 captchas solved, so you won't get rich this way, but if you're interested, here is a list of some of the best captcha sites to start with.

Kolotibablo—
http://kolotibablo.com/main/home
Mega Typers—
http://www.megatypers.com/register
Captcha Typers—to join Captcha Typers, you need to first send an email to aptchatypers@gmail.com. They will provide you with login details and any instructions you need to follow.
Pro Typers—
http://www.protypers.com/register

2Captcha—
https://2captcha.com/?from=974774
Qlinkgroup—
http://www.qlinkgroup.com/op/downlo
ad
PixProfit—pixprofit.com

It is very important that the information
and login details for joining a captcha
group are completely free. Do not
respond to anyone who asks you to pay
for these details, it is a scam.

Idea #18—Email Marketing

This one is very similar to affiliate
marketing with just a little difference.
With email marketing, you will have to
take your connections a little more
personally building strong bonds and
partnerships with both your merchant
and with your potential customers.

When you develop an email campaign,
you are informing them more as a friend
sharing good news about something that

will absolutely benefit them. You are in effect, selling them on a new idea or product, luring them to buy whatever the merchant is selling. For this type of job, it is necessary that you have at least some concept of marketing strategies and sales techniques. You must know when to give a hard-hitting pitch and when to hold back and take a gentler approach. This means you must know your target audience well and grow from there.

If you are an effective email marketer, you could easily collect thousands of dollars from a single email campaign. To get started, you can find jobs posted on sites like glassdoor.com, marketingcareeredu.org, or totaljobs.com.

Idea #19—Become a Survey Taker

There are many sites that will pay you to give them the information they need. By spending a few minutes each day taking surveys, you can generate a nice little passive income. While these surveys do not pay much, they can generate anywhere from $1 to $20 per survey, so if you're good at it, you can at least get some good pocket change. Here is a list of the top survey sites to get you started.

Global Test Market—https://www.globaltestmarket.com
Star Panel—http://www.tellypulse.com/
Toluna—https://in.toluna.com/#/
Brand Institute—http://www.brandinstitute.com/
Permission Research—https://www.permissionresearch.com/Home.aspx

Not all survey companies will accept you, so it is a good idea to apply at several. People are chosen based on where they live, age, gender, and financial status among other things.

Idea #20—Crowdfunding

Crowdfunding is a means by which people with a common goal pool their resources to sponsor a new business venture or cause of some kind. This allows individuals and businesses to compete on a larger scale than if they had to try to tackle an issue or need on their own.

It is also a great way for investors to gain a profit. Even if you only have a small sum to invest if worked right, you can build up a good return this way. The trick, however, is to choose an investment opportunity that has a good chance of succeeding. Many new businesses start every year, and there is also a real possibility that the one you choose to invest in will fail, so it is important to do good research and choose wisely. Still, with the right opportunity, you could make quite a bit of money with this type of investment tool.

The good news is that you don't have to start with a big outlay of cash. Many opportunities can be started with as little as $25. There are at least two sites you'll want to check out to get started.

Kickstarter—
https://www.kickstarter.com/
Kickfurther—
https://www.kickfurther.com/

Idea #21—Domain Trader

Trading domains can turn out to be quite a high-profit business strategy. You will need some investment capital to get started, and you'll also need to have a certain level of skill in creating domains and setting them up. You can purchase domains from sites like GoDaddy.com or other registrars. They are cheap and easy to sell, many you can get for around $10/name.

When a company can't find the right domain for their business, they will go directly to a domain trader to get it. As the trader, you get to fix the price for any domain under your control. There are lots of ways you can sell your domain names including auctioning them off. How much money you will make will depend on the prices you set and how many names you can purchase.

Idea #22—Offer a Web Search Service

This is probably one of the easiest ways of creating a passive income. You'll be getting paid for something you already do. Companies like Qmee.com offer you a monetary reward for doing research on Google, Bing, or Yahoo. All you do is simply install an add-on to your browser, and whenever you do any type of online research, you get a cash reward.

You accumulate cash until you are ready to cash out, and then, the money is sent directly to your PayPal account. Of course, there is an option for you to donate that money to charity if you would prefer, but the choice is completely yours.

There is an obvious advantage to this type of income; you'll be getting paid to do what you normally do anyway. It's easy, it's free, and there is nothing you must learn. If you're interested in this type of passive income, visit https://www.qmee.com to sign up and get started.

Idea #23—Review Music

This is a great idea for anyone who really loves music. By joining sites like Slicethepie.com, you can review new and unsigned musical artists online and get paid for your opinion.

The money you make will be slow in the beginning, but once you've built up a good reputation, you will have more people looking to you for your views on new music. Once you sign up, it is easy to get started. It is not difficult; all you do is listen to music and give your opinion, a great job for a true music lover.

Even though they are totally international, all money will be paid in US dollars. Anyone can sign up and create a review regardless of age, gender, or any other factors. Just head over to https://www.slicethepie.com/join/521823 and sign up to get started.

Idea #24—High-Interest Banking

If you have a little capital to get started, you can set up your own personal bank. Your income possibilities are endless with just a little investment in time to do adequate research setting up a high-interest bank account could be easy breezy.

Since banks no longer pay a high-interest rate for leaving your money in their care, it is not the best option for a store of cash. A better use of your money would be to create your own personal bank. Many companies like NetSpend, Consumers Credit Union, and others offer a better interest rate when you choose to deposit your money with them.

When setting up a savings account with these companies, you still need to be careful. Make sure that they have the right FDIC insurance and that their fees are within reason. Many may offer a better interest rate when you leave your money with them but will take it all back with high fees for monthly services or withdrawals.

Idea #25—Marketing Web Design Templates

There are millions of businesses right now that are online or are in the process of creating their own online presence, but most them do not have the skills to design their own website. If you have the skills to create Web Design Templates, you are in a good position to tap into this growing market.

Good web designers can easily rake in thousands of dollars a month by selling their newest designs. You will find that you can set your own price with some new businesses willing to pay as much a $100 for a precoded and predesigned template. It saves them the money of having to pay an expensive designer for the same service. The good news is that once your pages are designed, you can sell them repeatedly, and they can continue to generate money for you for years to come. Of course, you will want to freshen up your line from time to time so that you keep the interest coming back.

Getting started is a matter of first determining what you're good at and the right platform. It is best to start off with a few designs and then build up as you go. Once people can identify with your unique design style, you'll have a pretty good chance of success.

If you lack the designing skills in this area, you could always outsource the design work and buy it directly from an experienced designer and then post it online for sale.

There are several companies where you can sell your web design templates and start making money.

ThemeForest—https://themeforest.net
Templamatic—https://templatic.com/
BuyStockDesign—https://www.fantero.com/
Template Marketplace—https://flippa.com/?spm=1

Most people choose to purchase website templates because they don't know how, or they do not have the time to create their own website designs. This could be a highly lucrative market that once established could bring you a great deal of money.

Idea #26—Creating an App

Designing applications for the many different mobile devices has become big business these days. No matter where you are, who you are, or what you are, there is a good chance that you're using some type of application to get the things you want to be done. If you're in search of a highly lucrative opportunity and you have the skills to develop these apps, you are in a very enviable position.

The only thing you really need to know to get started is what people need. This means that you should expect to do a bit of market research so that you know exactly what type of application will have the most appeal to the public.

Once your application is designed, you can easily offer it in the Apple Store, Google Play, or another online store for sale. The good news is that the hard part is in the research. If you have the skills to create an application that can meet the needs of the public and simplify their time on their devices, you are good to go.

To do this, you will need at least some programming skills or the money to pay someone to do the programming for you. This could turn out to be easy money once it's all done and could generate income for many years if done well.

Idea #27—Online Investing

Another more advanced way to make money online is through online investing. With this method, you could generate a moderate income that could after a time, sustain you at the very least with a basic and steady flow of cash. There are many ways to invest online, including stocks, bonds, and forex trading. Other riskier investment options are also becoming very popular investment instruments.

You've probably already heard how investing in the stock market requires a large sum of upfront cash, but now there are several services that will let you get your foot in the door without having to shell out so much capital. In fact, some are willing to teach you how to invest with next to no capital investment of your own. Sites like Spark Profit at https://sparkprofit.com/ are even willing to go a step further to help you get started. With them, you do not even have to have any capital to put up. Just by making some predictions about what the market will do, you will get a score that can earn you money.

With every decision, you make you will earn points, the more points you get the more money you make. While you won't get a lot of money for your decisions, you will have something that you can then use to invest in the market and reap even bigger rewards all without having to shell out any capital of your own.

When it comes to deciding what to do with the stock market remember to follow the basic rules, buy low and sell high. It is not always easy to do, and you will have to learn how to read charts and graphs and analyze the market, but if you are good, there is quite a bit of money to be had. Whether you choose to invest in the stock market, mutual funds, ETFs, or something else, remember there is always a risk associated with each of these investments. Even the most experienced investors will lose from time to time to enter the market carefully and slowly so that you can gain more experience as you go.

For a consistent flow of income, consider investing in those ventures that pay dividends throughout the year.

Idea #28—Become an Influencer

Influencers are those people consumers look to before they decide to make a purchase. As more and more technology is developed, people are less likely to pay attention to promotional ads before deciding on a product or service. They usually will refer to those who have previously used the product and seek out their advice.

There are several ways you can set yourself up as an influencer. Most do YouTube videos reviewing certain products while others may insert their views through Facebook or Instagram. A popular influencer could easily generate a six-figure income with just a few videos. Even a lesser-known influencer can generate a stable income with the right audience.

Idea #29—Real Estate Investment Trusts

This is an easy way to get into real estate without purchasing real property to rent. You won't need to have a large amount of cash to invest in because you are merely purchasing "shares" in the real property.

There are several REITs you can invest in including residential, retail, industrial, office, hotel/resort, and storage.

Idea #30—Host Webinars

By hosting digital content that people are interested in you can generate a good sum of money. This may require a large investment in time from the very beginning, but after a while, this is a business that can easily begin to take care of itself. To be successful in this type of venture, make sure you find a topic that people will be keenly interested in. This means finding something that you could be excited about as well.

Once you have the right topic that appeals to both you and your target audience, build a website and start creating your content. The marketing efforts will be extensive in the beginning, but the better you are on the front end, the easier it will be later.

Idea #31—Article Writing

With the millions of websites already on Google, there is a lot of potential for profit in the article writing business. Every website must be regularly updated to keep their following interested. By offering your services as an article writer, you can supply these sites with fresh content on a regular basis. Many companies are more than willing to pay a nice sum for your services. It not only keeps their content fresh, but it saves them from having to come up with fresh ideas themselves.

To find these types of gigs, consider looking for sites that specifically need to kind of knowledge you already have. The fees you charge will depend a great deal on the topic, the audience, and the amount of time it could take to do the work. Reports have come in with some sites paying as little as $.20/word to as much as hundreds of dollars for a single blog post.

Below is a list of sites that are more than happy to pay for online articles.

Listverse
InstantShift
Freelancer Careers
IWriter
HubPages
Change Agent

Idea #32—Sell Products Through Online Auctions

One of the best places for bargain shopping is eBay. If you're good a scrounging around for good deals, you could pass those deals on to others by reselling items through eBay. Online auctions are becoming very popular today, and sites like eBay represent a pretty good way to give people exactly what they want at a price they can afford. The best eBay sellers will work to get ahead of the market by predicting what will be the next trends. If you're comfortable with taking a little risk and are willing to buy products in bulk, you can do well with this type of sales.

Idea #33—Multi-Level Marketing

This strategy allows you to generate income in two different ways. You can make commission by selling products yourself and generate a second stream by recruiting others to also sell products. With the second stream, you also draw commissions from the sales that your recruits make.

Make sure that if you try this avenue that you don't get involved in a pyramid scheme, which is illegal. It is also important to realize that these are not get-rich-quick schemes and that whatever product you plan to sell, there will be an initial investment that you will have to put up.

There are many companies that offer multilevel marketing opportunities; many of them offer the same products you use every day. Remember, the Internet is the replacement for door-to-door sales that were common in the past.

Idea #34—Cryptocurrencies

By now, almost everyone has heard about the crypto craze. Stories abound about people literally making fortunes overnight. It is true that there is money to be made in this type of venture, but before you jump in with both feet, it pays to do your research. This is a very new market, and things are very unpredictable, so enter this income stream at your own risk.

Everyone has heard of Bitcoin, but there are more than 1600 cryptocurrencies you can invest in. You must exercise extreme caution when investing in new coins because, in addition to the volatile market, many coins may not be able to compete in such a flooded market. For that reason, it is important for you to do more than the usual research when it comes to choosing the right coins to invest in.

Idea #35—Build Your Own Storefront

Profitable opportunities abound for online storefronts. There are several sites like Shopify or WooCommerce that make it easy to set up your own storefront to sell all sorts of products. You will need to obtain an SSL certificate and set up a way for your customers to accept payments, but once that is done, you are good to go.

You do not have to limit yourself to the products; you could also set up a storefront where you can provide consulting services directly from your site. All you need is a good website, a merchant account, and a target audience to market to.

Once it is set up, you can easily earn a sizable income from a regular stream of customers making it worth the initial hassles you will meet in getting started.

Idea #36—Testing Apps

There are many companies that will pay you for installing their apps on your mobile devices. You get paid for every month you use them. Check out sites like ShopTracker, Nielson Mobile Panel, and the MobileXpression. It only takes a few minutes to download the applications, answer a few questions and you're all set to start making money. Each of these sites will earn you about $50/year, and some will also reward you with prizes each week.

Idea #37—Earn Money for Maintaining Your Health

By using the health app AchieveMint, you can earn points for maintaining healthy practices. Every time you take a walk, keep track of your food intake, and make healthy choices in your life you accumulate points. These points can then be exchanged for Amazon Gift Cards, which you can use to purchase goods that can be used or sold for cash.

Idea #38—Private Tutoring

With great applications like FaceTime, Skype, Zoom, and others you can offer face to face classes that can earn you quite a bit of money. Some tutors are easily collecting as much as $50/hour for their services. Think of all the different ways students can benefit from your knowledge.

Students who are learning English, preparing for the SATs, or trying to master another skill you have will be more than willing to pay you for an hour of your time. You get to set your own schedule, choose which students you want to teach, and decide what subjects you want to offer. The ball is totally in your court, and you can collect as you go.

There will be a bit of marketing required in the beginning to get your name out, but once the ball starts rolling, you'll find that word of mouth will often be sufficient in keeping the money rolling in.

Idea #39—Sell Lesson Plans

If teaching is not your cup of tea but you have a lot of knowledge, you might want to sell your lesson plans. This is an ideal set-up because you only must create a plan once and then you can sell the same plans repeatedly. If your plans are good, you won't have any trouble getting busy teachers to pay money for them. It saves them both time and effort, and it can be a great benefit to the students as well.

Idea #40—Buy and Sell Used Books

All of us have books that we have read and have no intention of reading again. You can recycle books through websites like BookScouter—https://bookscouter.com, which connects you with used bookstore vendors where you can resell the books you collect. By buying back textbooks from students at the end of the year or just helping people get rid of their personal books that are cluttering up their house, you can generate quite a bit of income simply by serving as the middleman bringing people together with those vendors who are more than willing to take their used books off the shelf and put them in the hands of other people.

Conclusion

Thanks for making it through to the end of this book, let's hope it was informative and able to provide you with all the tools you need to achieve your goals whatever they may be.

So, there you have it. You now have 40 different ideas to generate passive income. Some of them are naturally very easy to get started, and some will require more skill and expertise. Depending on how much time and energy you want to put into the process, you could generate a very nice passive income that has the potential to free up your time and energy so that you can get back to living the life you really want to lead.

If you're willing to step outside of the box and try something new and different, there is money to be had regardless of your level of experience and knowledge. As our world continues to change and we become more tech savvy, it is only natural that more opportunities like these will arise. Why not start making money doing the things you are passionate about? That's the way it was for centuries, and it's only natural that we return to that concept of living.

One last thing, some of these plans may seem a bit complicated to get started, but if you persist, there is a good chance you can turn things around and find your way to financial independence. Even if you fail in one venture, don't hesitate to try another. Learn from your mistakes, and you'll soon see the fruits of your labors. It may take some time to get your plans off the ground, but once you do, you're as good as gold. Now, go out there and make some new money!

Finally, if you found this book useful in any way, a review on Amazon is always appreciated!

Description

All of us need extra cash now, and again, some of us more than others. Whether you're finally fed up with the drudgery of working for someone else and you're looking for more independence or you're just looking to build up some extra cash, there are lots of opportunities for you to find it online.

Through the pages of this book, you will learn how to set up and create your own online business showcasing your unique expertise. You'll learn how to do the following:

- Blog your way to a new income
- Set up your own eCommerce store
- Get paid for things you already do
- Teach classes online
- Or even write your own book

You'll learn all these things and so much more. Most people today have no idea how much money there is to be made through online channels, but after reading this book, you will. No matter how fast or how slow you want to go, you'll be able to tap into a wealth of information in the following pages. Information that can start you on your way to financial independence and a future where you are free to choose the kind of life you want and the kind of work you do.